Penguin

THE EXTRAORDINARY LIFE OF SERENA WILLIAMS

SHELINA JANMOHAMED

LEVEL

1

ADAPTED BY HANNAH FISH
ILLUSTRATED BY ASHLEY EVANS
SERIES EDITOR: SORREL PITTS

Some of the quotes in this book have been simplified
for learners of English as a foreign language.

PENGUIN BOOKS

UK | USA | Canada | Ireland | Australia
India | New Zealand | South Africa

Penguin Books is part of the Penguin Random House group of companies
whose addresses can be found at global.penguinrandomhouse.com.
www.penguin.co.uk www.puffin.co.uk www.ladybird.co.uk

Penguin
Random House
UK

The Extraordinary Life of Serena Williams first published by Puffin Books, 2020
This Penguin Readers edition published by Penguin Books Ltd, 2021
001

Original text written by Shelina Janmohamed
Text for Penguin Readers edition adapted by Hannah Fish
Text copyright © Shelina Janmohamed, 2020
Illustrated by Ashley Evans
Illustrations copyright © Ashley Evans, 2020
Additional illustrations (page 5: knee, Olympic rings, tennis court and racket)
by Alice Negri, copyright © Penguin Books Ltd, 2021
Cover image by Ashley Evans

The moral right of the original author and the original illustrator has been asserted

Printed and bound in Great Britain by Clays Ltd, Elcograf S.p.A.

The authorized representative in the EEA is Penguin Random House Ireland,
Morrison Chambers, 32 Nassau Street, Dublin D02 YH68.

A CIP catalogue record for this book is available from the British Library

ISBN: 978-0-241-49307-6

All correspondence to:
Penguin Books
Penguin Random House Children's
One Embassy Gardens, 8 Viaduct Gardens,
London SW11 7BW

Contents

People in the book

Serena Williams

Serena's sister Venus

Serena's father,
Richard

Serena's mother,
Oracene

Serena's husband,
Alexis

Serena's daughter,
Alexis Olympia

New words

knee

Olympic Games

tennis

tennis court

tennis racket

win

Note about the book

Tennis is a sport. **Successful*** tennis players are famous across the world and can make a lot of money. The Grand Slam **tournaments** are very important tennis tournaments, and all the great players play in them. There are four Grand Slams every year: Wimbledon in England, the French Open in France, the US Open in the USA, and the Australian Open in Australia.

Serena Williams is a famous tennis player. She is from the USA, but people across the world know her and love her.

Before-reading questions

1 Look at the title and cover of this book. What do you know about Serena Williams?

2 Which sport does Serena Williams play? What do you know about this sport?

3 Do you like sport? Which sports do you watch? Which sports do you play?

4 Which sports people are famous in your country?

*Defnitions of words in **bold** can be found in the glossary on pages 63–64.

CHAPTER ONE
Who is Serena Williams?

Serena Williams is a very **successful** tennis player. Many people say, "Serena Williams is the number-one **female** tennis player of all **time**."

But learning tennis was not easy for Serena. Her family did not have money for tennis lessons.

The Williams sisters

Serena had to play on old tennis courts, and her rackets and balls were very old.

Some people did not like Serena, because she was black. They said, "Black people do not play tennis!" But this **racism** did not stop Serena.

CHAPTER TWO
Serena the child

Serena was **born** on 26th September 1981 in Michigan, USA. Her father, Richard, and her mother, Oracene, had four more daughters – Yetunde, Lyndrea, Isha and Venus. Serena was the little sister. Serena loved her big sisters, and she was very close to Venus.

One day, Richard Williams watched tennis on television. He learned about tennis from books, and he and Oracene started teaching it to their daughters.

The Williams family **moved** to Compton, California, and lived in a small house. The five sisters had one bedroom with four beds.

Every day, the family played tennis. The courts were always dirty, and Richard had to clean them first.

Richard had to clean the courts.

Baby Serena watched her sisters, and then at three years old she started playing tennis, too. The family played tennis in the mornings and after school. They **practised** very hard.

Serena won many tennis **tournaments** for children. In 1991, Serena was ten years old, and her father talked to Rick Macci. Macci had a famous tennis **academy** in Florida.

Rick Macci

A **business** gave Serena and Venus some money. The family moved to Florida, and the girls started playing tennis at Rick Macci's academy.

Every day, after school, Serena and Venus went
to the academy and practised tennis for six hours.
They practised for six hours at the weekend, too.
This was very hard work.

After four years, Richard and Oracene started teaching Venus and Serena at home. Now, they could play more tennis, but schoolwork always came first. The girls liked a lot of different things – music, sports and reading.

Sadly, sometimes some white people at tennis tournaments said **horrible** things about Serena and Venus because they were black. Richard and Oracene were sad and angry about this racism, and the girls did not play in tournaments for the next four years.

In 1995, Serena was fourteen years old, and she started playing in tournaments again. This was an important year for Serena because she was now professional. Tennis was her job.

CHAPTER THREE

Serena the tennis player

Serena did not win her first professional **match**. She was now a student at a small school, and she had a lot of schoolwork.

Serena stopped playing in tennis tournaments for one more year, and she worked hard at school. She had a lot of friends at school, and they enjoyed playing games.

In 1997, Serena played her next professional match, but she did not win. She tried again and again. She worked hard, and she played good tennis. Then she started winning matches, and, at the **end** of 1997, she was in the world's top 100 female tennis players.

Sometimes Serena won, and sometimes she did not. But she always practised hard. In July 1998, she won her first Grand Slam tournament – Wimbledon – in the **doubles** with Max Mirnyi.

Serena with Max Mirnyi

Venus was now a very good tennis player, too, and sometimes Serena played her in matches. Serena loved her sister, but in a tennis match she always played hard. Venus often won their matches. Sometimes, the sisters played together in doubles matches. They loved this.

In September 1999, Serena won her first US Open tournament in the **singles**. She was now in the world's top ten female tennis players!

Serena worked hard at school, too, and, in the summer of 1999, she finished **high school**.

In 2001, Serena played in the Indian Wells tournament in California. Some people said horrible things about Serena because she was black.

Serena won the tournament, but she was sad and angry. She did not play at Indian Wells for the next fourteen years.

In June 2002, Serena won the French Open tournament, and then in July she won the Wimbledon tournament. Serena was very happy – she could not stop smiling! Now, she was the world's number-one female tennis player, and she was only twenty years old.

In 2002, Serena won Wimbledon.

In the years 2002 and 2003, Serena won all four Grand Slam tournaments. Only the great players can do this. In all these tournaments, Serena played Venus, and Serena won every match.

CHAPTER FOUR
Things get difficult

Serena was the world's number-one female tennis player, but things got **difficult** for her.

In 2002, Serena's parents **divorced**. Serena was not a child, but this was not easy for her. Then, in 2003, she had a problem with her knee. She was in hospital, and she could not play tennis.

Venus and Serena

In September 2003, Serena and her family got some horrible news. A man killed Serena's older sister Yetunde in Compton, California. Yetunde was only thirty-one years old and was the mother of three children. Serena was very sad.

Thinking about tennis was difficult for Serena now. She had to think about her family. And playing tennis was difficult because of her bad knee. In 2006, Serena was not in the world's top 100 female tennis players.

The families of many black Americans came to America from Africa. They did not want to come – they were **enslaved people**. In 2006, Serena travelled to Africa, and she learned about its people.

Serena helped people in Africa, too. She worked with **charities** and made schools for children in many African countries.

Serena was ready for tennis again. But some people said, "This is the end for Serena Williams. She cannot win tournaments, and she cannot be the world's number one again."

But Serena did not play tennis for those people. She played tennis because she loved it, and she loved winning. In 2007, she won the Australian Open tournament, and, in 2008, she was the world's number one again.

But things got difficult for Serena again. In the summer of 2010, she was in Germany. She walked on some glass and had to go to hospital.

Serena walked on glass.

Then, in 2011, she had a problem with her **lungs**, and she was in hospital again. Again people said, "Serena cannot play tennis now." But they were wrong. In only three months, Serena played in her next tennis tournament.

CHAPTER FIVE
Winning again

The next five years were very successful for Serena. In 2012, she won two **gold medals** at the Olympic Games in London – one in the singles, and one in the doubles with Venus. The same year, she won Wimbledon and the US Open.

In many sports, and in tennis, men and women do not make the same money. Serena was not happy about this. "Men and women must get the same!" she said.

Serena worked hard for female tennis players and for working women. Some of the big tournaments listened to her.

In 2014, she won the women's singles at the US Open, and Marin Čilić won the men's singles. Čilić got $3,000,000, and Serena got $3,000,000, too.

In 2015, Serena was in Rome. A man came and sat at her table at breakfast. His name was Alexis Ohanian.

Serena and Alexis started talking, and, that evening, Alexis watched Serena play at the Italian Open. After that, Serena and Alexis were often together, and today they are husband and wife.

In 2017, Serena was thirty-five. Some people said she was too old for a tennis player. But she worked hard and won more tournaments.

On 1st September 2017, Serena and Alexis had a baby daughter.

They gave their baby the name Alexis Olympia
Ohanian Junior. Alexis Olympia was born, and
then Serena had to go to hospital. She was not
well for six weeks.

Serena loved being a mum, but it was not easy, and she was very tired. Serena talked about the problems for mums and for working mums.

Going back to tennis was difficult for Serena. She was now number 451 in the world. But she worked hard, and, in 2018, she came second at Wimbledon.

CHAPTER SIX
Serena the woman

At twenty years old, Serena Williams was number one in the world, and she was number one again at thirty-five years old. She has twenty-three Grand Slam wins and four Olympic gold medals. But Serena does not only play tennis.

Serena loves clothes and **fashion**. After high school, she went to the Art Institute at Fort Lauderdale. She learned about fashion, and, in 2004, she started her own fashion business.

Clothes are important for Serena, and her body is important for her, too. You can see photos of Serena in the news, and in sport and fashion books. She is happy with her clothes and with her body. Sometimes, people say horrible things about Serena's body, but she does not listen to them.

Serena is happy with her body.

Helping people is important for Serena, too. She helps women, black people, and young people with their new businesses, and she works with many charities.

Serena is often on television, and she writes books and for the news.

So, what is next for Serena Williams? She loves playing tennis, and she loves being a mum. She loves helping people, and she loves working hard. This is not the end of her story.

During-reading questions

CHAPTER ONE

1 What do many people say about Serena Williams?
2 Learning tennis was not easy for Serena. Why?
3 Some people did not like Serena. Why?

CHAPTER TWO

1 Who started teaching the sisters about tennis?
2 Why did the family move to Florida?
3 Why did Serena and Venus stop going to school?
4 What made Richard and Oracene sad?

CHAPTER THREE

1 Did Serena win her first professional match?
2 What did Serena win in July 1998?
3 What did Serena and Venus love doing?
4 What did some people say at the Indian Wells tournament in 2001?
5 In 2002, Serena was the world's number-one female tennis player. How old was she?

CHAPTER FOUR

1 Why was Serena in hospital in 2003?
2 How did Serena's sister Yetunde die?
3 What did Serena do in Africa?
4 Why was Serena in hospital in 2010?

CHAPTER FIVE

1 How many Olympic gold medals did Serena win in 2012?
2 Who did Serena work hard for?
3 Who is Serena's husband?
4 Does Serena like being a mum?

CHAPTER SIX

1 What business did Serena start in 2004?
2 Where can you see photos of Serena?
3 Who does Serena help with their new businesses?
4 What does Serena love doing?

After-reading questions

1 Serena is a tennis player, but she does a lot more.
What does she do?

2 Was Serena's early life easy or difficult? Why?

3 Why is Serena successful, do you think?

4 What do you think about Serena's mother and father?

Exercises

1 **Write short answers to these questions in your notebook.**

1 Is Serena Williams a successful tennis player? .....*Yes, she is*.....

2 Was learning tennis easy for Serena?

3 Did Serena's family have money for tennis lessons?

4 Were Serena's rackets and balls very old?

5 Did some people say, "Black people do not play tennis!"?

6 Did this racism stop Serena?

2 **Complete these sentences in your notebook, using the words from the box.**

born	horrible	academy	professional
business	tournaments	moved	

1 Serena was ....*born*.......... on 26th September 1981 in Michigan, USA.

2 The Williams family .... to Compton, California.

3 Serena won many tennis .... for children.

4 Rick Macci had a famous tennis .... in Florida.

5 A .... gave Serena and Venus some money, and the family moved to Florida.

6 Sometimes people said .... things about Serena and Venus.

7 In 1995, Serena was .... – tennis was her job.

CHAPTER THREE

3 **Complete these sentences in your notebook. Use the past simple of the verbs in brackets.**

1 Serena ......*stopped*...... (**stop**) playing in tennis tournaments for one year.

2 Serena .... (**work**) hard, and she played good tennis.

3 Venus .... (**be**) a very good tennis player, too.

4 In September 1999, Serena .... (**win**) the US Open tournament.

5 Serena .... (**do**) not play at Indian Wells for fourteen years.

6 Serena was very happy. She .... (**can**) not stop smiling.

7 Serena .... (**play**) Venus, and she won every match.

CHAPTER FOUR

4 **Are these sentences *true* or *false*? Write the correct answers in your notebook.**

1 Things were always easy for Serena. ....*false*............

2 Serena's parents divorced in 2002.

3 Serena's sister Yetunde had four children.

4 The families of many black Americans came to America from Europe.

5 Serena came back from Africa and did not play tennis again.

6 In 2008, Serena was the world's number one again.

7 In 2011, Serena had a problem with her lungs.

5 **Choose the correct form of the verb to complete these sentences in your notebook.**

Example: 1 – b

1 The next five years .... very successful for Serena.

   a was   **b** were   **c** being

2 In many sports, men and women do not .... the same money.

   a make   **b** makes   **c** making

3 At breakfast, a man .... and sat at Serena's table.

   a is coming   **b** comes   **c** came

4 On 1st September 2017, Serena and Alexis .... a baby daughter.

   a having   **b** had   **c** have

5 Serena loved being a mum, but she .... very tired.

   a being   **b** were   **c** was

6 Serena .... hard, and, in 2018, she came second at Wimbledon.

   a worked   **b** works   **c** is working

6 **Choose the correct word to complete these sentences in your notebook.**

1 Serena loves clothes and *fashion* / **academies**.

2 Serena is happy with her clothes and with her **high school** / **body**.

3 Serena helps people with their new **tournaments** / **businesses**.

4 Serena works with many **charities** / **hospitals**.

5 Serena is often on **trains** / **television**, and she writes books.

6 This is not the **end** / **time** of Serena's story.

7 Write about these people in your notebook.

Serena Williams

Venus Williams

Richard Williams

Oracene Williams

Alexis Ohanian

Alexis Olympia
Ohanian Junior

Example:

Her name is Serena Williams. She is a tennis player,
a mother and a businesswoman.

Project work

1 Imagine you are Serena Williams at ten years old. Write a one-week diary page about that time.

2 Serena Williams lived in California and Florida in the USA. Look online, and find out more about one of these places. Make a poster about it.

3 In many sports, men and women do not make the same money. Serena was angry about this, and she said, "All players must get the same!"

   Do you agree with Serena? Write a letter to her and say what you think.

4 There are four grand slam tournaments:
   a Wimbledon
   b the French Open
   c the US Open
   d the Australian Open
   Look online, and find out more about one of these tournaments. Make a presentation about it.

5 Write about this book. Did you like it? Why/Why not?

An answer key for all questions and exercises can be found at **www.penguinreaders.co.uk**

Glossary

academy (n.)
a school. A tennis *academy* teaches people how to play tennis well.

born (v.)
A baby comes out from its mother's body. It is *born*.

business (n.)
A *business* buys and sells things.

charity (n.)
A *charity* helps people in need. Many people give money to *charities*.

difficult (adj.)
not easy

divorce (v.)
A husband and wife *divorce*, and then they are not together.

doubles (n.)
There are four people in a *doubles* tennis *match*.

end (n.)
Something finishes at the *end*.

enslaved people (n.)
Enslaved people work very hard for no money.

fashion (n.)
nice clothes and shoes. People want to wear them.

female (adj.)
A girl or woman is *female*.

gold medal (n.)
You are first in a *tournament*, and then you get a *gold medal*. A *medal* is a small metal thing.

high school (n.)
People go to *high school* between thirteen and eighteen years old. There are *high schools* in America.

horrible (adj.)
very bad

lungs (n.)
Your *lungs* are inside the top part of your body. They help you to take air into and out of your body.

match (n.)
an important game of tennis

move (v.)
to go to a different place and live there

practise (v.)
You do something a lot, and then you can do it well. You *practise*.

racism (n.)
Racism is believing that some groups of people are better than others.

singles (n.)
There are two people in a *singles* tennis *match*.

successful (adj.)
You do something well and then you get money or things, and sometimes you are famous. You are *successful*.

time (n.)
all the minutes, hours, days, weeks, months and years

tournament (n.)
In a *tournament*, people play a lot of games. The winners (= the best or first people in games) play games with other winners. After all these games, there is one winner of the *tournament*. This is because they were the best in every game.